"Big GOD" is a book for all ages young and old, helping them get a glimpse of what God can do, and showing what to do, and what not to do. Even if you already know what to do, and what not to do. This book will still help you and your relationship with God and people.

GIFT PAGE

To: _____

From: _____

Date: _____

Occasion: _____

Other:

_____

_____

_____

_____

All scriptures are from the KJV version of the Bible, unless specified otherwise.
Book & Cover Design by Samaria Dixon
Cover Photo by Lynda Maupin
BIG GOD discussions for today's youth

BIG GOD

Copyright©2013 by Samaria Dixon

All rights reserved under international Copyright Law. This publication may not be reproduced, stored in a retrieval system, or transmitted in whole or part in any form of means, electronic, photocopying, or otherwise, without prior express permission of writer or publisher.

Introduction

God bless you in your journey of realizing how amazing and special you are… not only in the eyes of people you may not know, but most importantly, God. You can begin your journey at any age young or old, it doesn't matter how old you are!!! I hope that you're truly blessed by this book and that it strengthens your relationship with God. Enjoy!!!

I love you...

To Jesus, Thank You so much for enabling me to do this book!!! Thank you Jesus!!!

To my mom who is truly the best mom in the universe. I love you so much!!! You are the B.E.S.T MOM IN THE UNIVERSE!!! THANK YOU SO MUCH FOR SUPPORTING me!!! I love you !!!!!!!!!!!!!

THANK YOU MOMMY

To my brother who is truly the best brother in the universe.

I LOVE YOU SO MUCH!!! B.E.S.T BROTHER EVER !!!

To my sisters I love you so much!!!

To my best friends!!! I love you all in the Lord!!!!!

GOD BLESS YOU!!!

To my niece who I love to call my best friend and sister! ☺ I hope this book will help you when you learn how to read! I LOVE YOU JESUS!!! THANK YOU God!!!

-GOD BLESS YOU ALL-

God has a plan

God has a plan for your life, sometimes it may not seem like it, but He really does!!! God will never give up on you or me. He will always be right by your side helping you along the way. God has a plan for your life… you just watch and see!!! ☺ God is so, so, so, so, so, good and there are a LOT more so's where that came from!!!

THANK YOU GOD… GLORY HALLELUJAH!!!

God, you have shown me one of the purposes in my life.

God is love

Think about what the Lord has done for you today… He woke you up this morning and started you on your way!!! Isn't He good!!! Don't you love Him!!! He sent His one and only son to die on the cross for all of our sins!!! He woke you up this morning and you are still breathing right now!!!

Now that's just amazing!!! And if you think that is amazing, then wait until I tell you this… The blessings aren't near done like my mom says … "As long as you have breath flowing in and out of your lungs you still have purpose", and I add as long as you have breath flowing in and out of your lungs, there is still a purpose for you and in you. Thank you Jesus HALLELUJAH!!! And since I know that is not all that He has done for you today, on the lines below write about what God has done for you today… God loves you so much remember to keep him first in everything that you do!!!

Write about it

On the lines below write about some of the things that God has done for you today.

_____
_____
_____
_____
_____
_____
_____
_____
_____

Isaiah 53:5

"...He was wounded for our transgressions, he was bruised for our iniquities: the chastisement of our peace was upon him; and with his stripes we are healed."

Deuteronomy 28
Blessings

And it shall come to pass, if thou shalt hearken diligently unto the voice of the Lord thy God, to observe and to do all his commandments which I command thee this day, that the Lord thy God will set thee on high above all nations of the earth:

2 And all these blessings shall come on thee, and overtake thee, if thou shalt hearken unto the voice of the Lord thy God.

3 Blessed shalt thou be in the city, and blessed shalt thou be in the field.

4 Blessed shall be the fruit of thy body, and the fruit of thy ground, and the fruit of thy cattle, the increase of thy kine, and the flocks of thy sheep.

5 Blessed shall be thy basket and thy store.

6 Blessed shalt thou be when thou comest in, and blessed shalt thou be when thou goest out.

7 The Lord shall cause thine enemies that rise up against thee to be smitten before thy face: they shall come out against thee one way, and flee before thee seven ways.

⁸ The LORD shall command the blessing upon thee in thy storehouses, and in all that thou settest thine hand unto; and he shall bless thee in the land which the LORD thy God giveth thee.

⁹ The LORD shall establish thee an holy people unto himself, as he hath sworn unto thee, if thou shalt keep the commandments of the LORD thy God, and walk in his ways.

¹⁰ And all people of the earth shall see that thou art called by the name of the LORD; and they shall be afraid of thee.

¹¹ And the LORD shall make thee plenteous in goods, in the fruit of thy body, and in the fruit of thy cattle, and in the fruit of thy ground, in the land which the LORD sware unto thy fathers to give thee.

¹² The LORD shall open unto thee his good treasure, the heaven to give the rain unto thy land in his season, and to bless all the work of thine hand: and thou shalt lend unto many nations, and thou shalt not borrow.

¹³ And the LORD shall make thee the head, and not the tail; and thou shalt be above only, and thou shalt not be beneath; if that thou hearken unto the commandments of the LORD thy God, which I command thee this day, to observe and to do them.

Notes on this book

_____

_____

_____

_____

_____

_____

_____

_____

_____

_____

NAMES OF GOD...

Lily of the valley, the Beginning, And The End, Jehovah Nissi, Prince of Peace, Alpha And Omega. Can you think of any other names of God?...

Of course you can. There are over 100's of names of God!!! ☺

Write about it!!!

On the lines below think of some of the names of God and write them down.

_____
_____
_____
_____

God Is …

The Alpha and the Omega, the Beginning and the End… and no one can come unto the father but by Him.

God is...

Loving, Kind, Amazing, and more!!!... ABLE!!!

God…

God THE Healer, Provider, Protector, Deliverer, Maker and Warrior.

Proverbs 1:1-9

1 The proverbs of Solomon the son of David, king of Israel;

2 To know wisdom and instruction; to perceive the words of understanding;

3 To receive the instruction of wisdom, justice, and judgment, and equity;

4 To give subtilty to the simple, to the young man knowledge and discretion.

5 A wise man will hear, and will increase learning; and a man of understanding shall attain unto wise counsels:

⁶ To understand a proverb, and the interpretation; the words of the wise, and their dark sayings.

⁷ The fear of the LORD is the beginning of knowledge: but fools despise wisdom and instruction.

⁸ My son, hear the instruction of thy father, and forsake not the law of thy mother:

⁹ For they shall be an ornament of grace unto thy head, and chains about thy neck.

The Fourth of July Liberty to be me...

On the fourth of July we (my mom, my little brother, and I) ran the Bluegrass 10,000 race. It was soooo fun. I thank GOD for helping us accomplish it. We might have been late starting the race, but like my mom always says, "It is **not** how you start but *that* YOU **FINISH**!!!" I thought that most people had left, but there were still people cheering us on. I was so happy and even though I took a three hour nap after a six mile run, I felt awesome! (kind of)! ☺ So even though we didn't win the Bluegrass 10,000 race, we got a lot more power… where that came from!!! ☺THANK YOU GOD!!! HALLELUJAH!!!!

The Power of the Tongue

Think about it...If your words were powerful, (which they are) is there anything that you would change that you might have said in the past? Substitute anything that you might have said that might have been slightly bad, for something good... like say the opposite instead!

So from now on I want you to think about the words that you are about to say you are going to say because once you have spoken them out you can't take them back.

GOD IS GOOD!!!

God is good, he provides us with everyday manna!

Can you imagine if God had second thoughts about sending His one and only son (who knew No sin) to earth to die for our sins? Can you imagine sending your one and only child to die on the cross for every single person's sins?
Think about it! You're in heaven where there is absolutely No sin, No pain, and No sorrow, then your father sends you down to earth (the #1 planet of sin and destruction☹) to give everyone a choice of heaven or hell. So there you are on the cross died for everybody else's sins! God is so good he sent his one and only son to die for everybody else's sins! But then something marvelous happens...Jesus rose from the dead to show the Lords power! (Well, that's only one reason!)☺

Peace

My mom always says that the peacemaker shall inherit the earth. It is very important not to stir up anger or do anything unpleasing to God. Why? Because God told us not to break His laws. We are, as Christians, supposed to build each other up, encouraging thy brethren in Christ! THANK YOU GOD HALLELUJAH!!!!

Did You Know?

Did you know that the bible gives instructions not to spoil children? Because if your parents spoil you…that (most likely) means that it will not help to train you up in the way that you should go. Meaning that if your parents spoil you, then you won't be ready for what the world will bring as you start growing up. So don't be mad when your parents punish you. They're only trying to protect you. So even punishments and "take-a-ways" are necessary to mold us into good people, and… to prepare us for the world. So don't think that they hate you or anything… They love you enough to look after you and care for you…and I think that's pretty cool! ☺

THE LORD'S PRAYER

Our father, who art in heaven, holy be Thy name, Thy kingdom come, Thy will be done, on earth, as it is in heaven, Give us this day our daily bread, forgive us our debts, as we forgive our debtors, lead us not into temptation and deliver us from evil, for thine is the kingdom, and the power and the glory, Forever, AMEN.

IF GOD IS FOR US WHO CAN BE AGAINST US?

If God is for us, who can be against us! When I think about this I feel comforted. So what that means is... If God is with us, then not only will we never be alone...but also we don't have to worry about people not treating us right or anything like that. God will always be with you...looking out for us, and taking up for us. He will never leave you nor forsake you. Sometimes you might think that you're all alone, but you're not. It is only a test, and if you past the test you will truly be blessed. You are one of God's children, and God loves you very much! So remember that you are very special, and that God loves you very much, and has a very special plan for your life!!! ☺

I believe ...

"I believe that we can make a difference, one small act at a time..."
~Lynda Maupin~

"I believe that we can make a difference, one small act at a time..."

The way we can is by spreading God's love throughout the nation...

When we tell people about the love of God, and tell people to spread it around in a way that it will affect people, then we can truly make a difference.

When we build each other up, building up our fellow brethren, encouraging, inspiring, making a difference, *then* I believe that we are impacting the lives of our brothers and sisters in Christ... and I believe that *then* we are impacting the lives of people other than the people that we helped... they will start to do what we did...

building up, inspiring, encouraging and helping each other find our purpose for God...and I believe that it is *then* that we are making our first or maybe more acts of kindness...and I believe that it is *then* when we make our first act of history.

Thank you Jesus!!!

~Samaria Dixon~

Book Quiz

What have you learned

_____

_____

_____

_____

_____

_____

Has this book inspired you?

_____

_____

_____

_____

_____

_____

_____

_____

_____

Do you think that this book will help you in your everyday life? And how so?

_____
_____
_____
_____
_____
_____
_____
_____
_____
_____
_____
_____
_____

SEEK THE LORD

In the Bible it says, "Seek the Lord and all these things will be added unto you." So what that means is when you are striving hard to obey the Lord, and I mean really trying, pushing, and pressing. Then all your dreams according to God's will, will be added unto you.

Isn't that great!... So when we keep the laws of the land, and God's law, then God will bless you and give you more for whatever you gave up for the Lord. "What would it profit a man to gain the world and lose their soul?" And what that, my friend means is, if you gain earthly riches, and you're not saved, then all your riches will not matter. So I tell you let God come into your heart! Ask him to forgive your sins, repent and turn away from your sins! and you **will be made new!!! Thank you God hallelujah**

Being a Christian God gives me…

Being a Christian gives me… Joy, peace, confidence, love, patience, kindness, gentleness, and meekness. And how fitting, because that's just a glimpse of things that come from the Lord and when you have Him in you! ☺ Let the words of my mouth and the meditation of my heart, be acceptable in thy sight, O Lord, my strength, and my redeemer. –PSALM 19:14

GOD IS AWESOME

I know that I have already talked about this before in this book, but I'm gonna say it again with a few changes.

Think about what he has done for you today, He woke you up this morning and started you on your way, just think about what He is doing for you right now… Isn't God good!!! ☺ He sent His one and only son to die on the cross for our sins, He woke you up this morning and you're alive and well right now!!! Isn't God good?!! Just watch how God is going to bless you today, tomorrow, and all the years to come. From the rising of the sun unto the going down of the same the Lord's name is to be praised. The Lord is high above all nations, and HIS GLORY above all the nations, and His glory above the heavens. – Psalm 113:3-4

Think About It...

What has the Lord done for you today? (hint) you can't write down *everything* that God has done for you. I'm just asking that you write down a few more things.

_____
_____
_____
_____
_____
_____
_____
_____

DEAR GOD,
I love You, thank You, praise You, magnify You, and glorify You.
Thank You for what You have done for me, and are going to do for me.
AMEN.

True sayings

1-WITH God all things are possible

2-When you walk with God you will Always reach your destination

3-God is always with you and for you

4-Don't ever give up on God because He'll never give up on you (He's able!)

5-Our God IS an awesome God There is none like thee. ☺

One thing that I want to do one day…

I have been cooking since I was 9 years old, and I enjoy it so much. I learned from the best, my mom. I love being able to try different things, cooking for my family and friends! ☺. One thing that I want to do one day, is go on Food Network, either competitively or just to have my own show.

I have lots of new and different ideas on how to make just about anything and everything. And though cooking is not the biggest thing that I'm interested in, (singing and acting are) I still love it, and I am going to use every one of my talents known and not yet known, to the best of my abilities, bringing glory to GOD'S name!!!

I strongly encourage you to do the same. Find what you're good at, then do it unto the best of your abilities. Bringing glory to God's name, the one that put the talent in you. You might not know your talent yet, but God will show you in due time.

What are some of the things you want to do someday?...

_____
_____
_____
_____
_____
_____
_____
_____
_____
_____
_____

Note pages

What did you think of this book? Love it?! Great!

Other products and books coming soon.

Also check these AMAZING books out…

Along the Way- by Lynda Maupin

And

Let's Talk About GOD- by Emmanuel Dixon

These two amazing books are for everyone, young and old!... and they were written by two very special people… My Mom and My Little Brother!!! And are coming to a store near you!!!

Thank you for your love and support in helping us spread the gospel in little ways! Follow us on Facebook

@Lynda Maupin

@Children of Purpose

Samaria Dixon & Emmanuel Dixon